How to Write Your Nonfiction Book
Andrew Lawrence

About the author

Andrew Lawrence is the author of 20 nonfiction inspirational self-help books. His books include:

Step It Up: The Quest For Success

Life Changers: 10 true secrets that will change your life

The Happiness Transformation

Discover Your Life Purpose in 30 Minutes

MONEY - The Basics

Stories Of A Lifetime (biography)

How To Get A Job

Beat Your Fatigue

The 65-Year-Old Teenager

How To Thrive After 65

Wall Street - The Real Deal

Free excerpts at
  https://Andrew-Lawrence.blogspot.com

How To Write
Your Nonfiction Book
A guide for the nonfiction author

by

Andrew Lawrence

© 2017

Name: How To Write Your Nonfiction Book

ISBN-10: 1543085628

EAN-13: 978-1543085624

Printer: CreateSpace

Color: B/W with No Bleed

Country of Publication: United States

Author: Andrew Lawrence

Cover Design : Andrew Lawrence

Proofreading: Muriel Hufman

Table Of Contents

Andrew Lawrence

Why I wrote this book

Where do I get my ideas for my books? From people around me. People who want to improve their life but are having difficulty doing it. I want to help. And I'm good at it. And I realize that, besides that one individual, many other people may have the same problems improving their life, proceeding with their dreams. If feasible, sometimes I write a book helping them to do it.

If I sell only one book that helps a person improve their life it will have been worthwhile writing it.

I wrote THIS book because a friend of mine wanted to write a nonfiction book about her grandmother in early Alaska and her family's important part in the development of that state. My friend is a female Jewish Eskimo. One of the few female Jewish Eskimos in the world. I realized that, in a good way, she is an unusual person and this is an unusual book – an unusual book that deserves to be written – an unusual book that falls under the categories of American history, Alaskan history, biography, early women's rights, Eskimos, and Jewish Eskimos. WOW! That's Nobel Prize worthy!

After 10 years she informed me that she was ready to write the book. Besides supporting the effort, I also realized that it would be Muriel's first book and she may not know how to write it, or how to proceed. Having written 20 nonfiction books myself I decided to help her - and others - by writing a beginner's guide to writing a nonfiction book. Hence this book. I hope it helps her. And you.

Regards,

Andrew Lawrence
Los Angeles, CA
February 1, 2017

Every author who ever lived had to write
their first book

Introduction

So you want to write a book? That sounds like a good idea, a great idea, a worthy goal, a dream. Or a fantasy. Thinking about writing a book, dreaming about it – and doing it – are very different. Thinking about it is like singing in the shower. Writing it and putting it out for the world to see is like singing on stage, in front of an audience.

Beginning writers can have stage fright. Feelings of unworthiness, and/or suffer from a lack of experience or know-how. It can be overwhelming. These are normal feelings. Lousy but normal. Feelings which can stop you from writing your book. Don't let them. Write your book!

The purpose of this book – and all my books - is to motivate, stimulate and educate. That also applies to writing a nonfiction book.

Want to write a book? Here's how to proceed ....

First and Foremost

The first thing about writing a nonfiction book is to have something worth writing about. Preferably something of interest to YOU and hopefully of interest to others. Why is that important? Because writing a book is not easy; it's difficult and frustrating and takes time. Being passionate about your subject matter makes it easier to overcome the obstacles of organizing, writing, rewriting, editing and re-editing, not to mention publishing. No, don't get discouraged. You CAN write your book! You WILL write your book.

The objective of this book is to get you to write, and finish, your manuscript. It's called the First Draft.

My objective in this book is not to help you learn how to write, how to get your manuscript published, or how to promote your book or become a bestselling author. The objective of this book is to help you do your nonfiction book. First, you have to write it. And then you have to finish it. THAT is the focus of this book.

Motivation

Why do you want to write your book? Yes, it's important to know why. If you aren't sure, or don't know, ask yourself, "Why am I writing this book?" To get rich? To become famous? To have people like and admire you? To educate? To impart wisdom? To honor something or someone? To help yourself and improve your life? To help others? It is a good thing to know why you are motivated to write your book. I write my books to help others improve their life. Why do you want to write YOUR book?

I wrote my first book, "Stories Of A Lifetime" (extraordinary events in an extraordinary life) for purely selfish reasons. During my lifetime I have had numerous unusual, incredible things happen to me. Extraordinary things. Magical things. My real life true stories include, "A Case of ESP", "The Night We Saw A Real UFO", "Man Kills Building" and "The Eight-Million-Dollar Mistake". These are truly incredible true stories. And, incredibly, they happened to ME. If they didn't actually happen to me I would never have believed they happened!

Here's why I wrote that book. I was no longer young, and realized that someday I might become old and senile, and would not be able to remember any of the wonderful amazing things I witnessed, or that were part of my life. I decided to write them all down. So I could someday read them. I had fantastic memories – MY memories - and I did not ever want to lose them. I did it. I wrote the book. And I realized that, not only were the amazing stories interesting to read – they were inspirational. I ended up writing the book not only for myself but as life inspiration for others. The inspirational message was : "Make memories. Make them now. Make them glorious!"

That inspiration also applies to you - and your book. Make a memory. Make your book. Make it now. Make it glorious!

How Old Should You Be?

How old should you be to write a book? As old as you are. There are teenage authors, 20-30 something authors, 50-60 year old authors and old, really old, authors. Age is just a number. If you have something to say or share, and feel compelled to say or share in print, be an author.

How old should you be to be an author? Here's some examples (fictional authors and non-fictional authors):

When he was twelve years old, Florida-based Jake Marcionette released his debut book, "Just Jake", a loosely autobiographical, laugh-out-loud comedy adventure. With that book Jake became the youngest author to hit the New York Times Bestseller list

Alexander Pope wrote his first poem, "Ode to Solitude," at the age of 12. It was in the year 1700

Helen DeWitt published "The Last Sumarai" at 41

The Marquis De Sade wrote his first book in prison, at the age of 42

Bram Stoker didn't write "Dracula" until he was 50

Raymond Chandler published "The Big Sleep" at 51

Millard Kaufman published his first novel at the age of

90

Bertha Wood (UK) had her first book, "Fresh Air and Fun: The Story of a Blackpool Holiday Camp" published on her 100th birthday

Writers write. At any age and every age. Age is just a number. Write your book!

Hurry Up and Wait

After the idea for "the greatest book ever written" pops into your head, don't run and start writing it. Wait. Write down the idea (or a title). And then, wait for the initial excitement and elation to subside. Why not start writing it right away? Because every book is not worth writing. Every idea does not convert into a book. When you get a great idea for a book – wait. Think about it for a few days. I wait 3 days or so. Then, after 3 days, if the idea is still valid, if I think I can turn the idea into a book, I proceed to the next step. Very often, the book idea I have turns out to not be such a good idea for a book. Yes, it's disappointing. Yes, it's part of writing. I have 6 incomplete unwritten books which started out with a great idea; only to be tabled for a variety of good and valid reasons. One book was a wonderfully inspiring poetry book. The problem is that I know nothing about writing poetry. I wrote a dozen short poems over several weeks and then went dry. The book is unwritten. The other books were so subjective that they ended up being nearly impossible to write. These are what I call non-books, ideas which turned out not to be books. When I started turning each of these 6 ideas into a book, I quickly discovered that I couldn't organize and write the information in a way that could be easily understood by the reader. The subject matter of those non-books was just too subjective, and sometimes, too spiritual and too hard to follow. That is not good for a self-help author like me. I still have the titles and covers and did some writing on those books and maybe someday I will be able to continue, and finish, writing them. Or not. Welcome to being an author.

Every idea is not a book. It takes quite a bit of time to write a book so it pays to wait a few days or weeks and think about it and determine if your book is worth writing. Or, if it CAN be written.

The good news is that, even if a book ends up to be not worth writing, the idea and subject matter is initially often so exciting and stimulating, that in, and of itself, it's good for you!

What If You Can't Write?

Lots of people are not good at writing. In fact, lots of people are truly lousy at writing.

What do you do if you want to write a book but can't write well? How do you write a book on a computer if you are computer illiterate? Write it anyway. You can use other ways to tell your story. Write it on paper, using a pen or pencil. Dictate it if you are more comfortable speaking rather than writing. When you're done find someone to transcribe your words onto a computer (onto paper). Or find a co-author or someone and TELL your story and have THEM write it down.

Lots of authors do not write well. It may seem easier to write a book if a writer can actually write, but don't let that stop you from doing your book!

Lots of people can't do math either. It doesn't mean they are stupid, it just means their brains are just not wired to do math. Same with writing. Some of the smartest and most successful people on the planet couldn't write a proper sentence or were dyslexic. If they had to write something they found someone to write it for them. Including books.

As for me, I was always good in English. Since I was 10

years old I enjoyed reading books, lots of books. That's how I learned how to write. By reading. I also learned to write from Ernest Hemingway. What? Ernest Hemingway? Really? No, not from him personally. From reading his great books. He wrote simply, clearly and strongly. And when asked the secret of his fabulous writing style he said, "Use only enough words to tell the story – and no more". I have followed his advice in all 20 of my nonfiction books.

Yes, I can write and I'm somewhat computer literate. But I can't type. I hunt and peck on my laptop keyboard with my two index fingers. Sometimes with just one finger. I'm slow as hell and I make a LOT of mistakes. But I get the job done. So can you!

Fiction versus Nonfiction

Fiction and nonfiction are very different. I should know; once upon a time I tried to write a book of fiction and failed miserably. I was defeated as soon as I got started. Why? Because writing a fiction book requires a lot of creative **imagination** – and I didn't have enough of it. I am analytical and naturally like to organize ideas (and facts) and present them – in order to help others improve their lives. That's who I am. That's why I'm here. That's why I write nonfiction.

Fiction on the other hand tells a story. A made-up story. Writing fiction involves a plot, characters, dialogue, action and other unique things. It is a descriptive medium. Most fictional books have a lot of "detail", verbally describing surroundings, interiors and exteriors, action, emotions, etc. Nonfiction books often do not have all those things. They are "non fiction, not fiction". According to Dictionary.com nonfiction is: "the branch of literature comprising works of narrative prose dealing with or offering opinions or conjectures upon facts and reality, including biography, history, and the essay."

Can a writer write both fiction and nonfiction? Maybe. I don't know. I know I can't. Maybe you can.

Nonfiction

According to Nielsen (the ratings company): "non-fiction was the highlight of 2015 (the latest year I could find), with 12% growth in children's non-fiction and 7% growth in adult non-fiction."

According to Publishers Weekly, the top 10 nonfiction books of 2016 were:

Killing the Rising Sun (Bill O'Reilly) sold over 1 million copies

The Life-Changing Magic of Tidying Up

The Magnolia Story

Strengths Finder 2.0

Jesus Calling

When Breath Becomes Air

Born to Run (Bruce Springsteen)

Milk and Honey

Alexander Hamilton

You Are a Badass

There are many different subjects covered in these and other nonfiction books. Life. Death. History. Biography. Religion. Self-help. There are two general categories of nonfiction. According to book editor Jessi Hoffman, they are: "research nonfiction and creative nonfiction. Research nonfiction is straight factual writing. Essentially, it means journalism (the kind of stuff you find in the newspapers). Creative nonfiction, by contrast, is any writing that embellishes facts.... (Examples would be the genres of memoir and the personal essay.) Creative fiction is also sometimes called literary nonfiction or narrative nonfiction." No, you don't have to remember all that. Whew!

What are YOU writing about?

Which nonfiction category does your book fall into? Common genres include:

Biography/autobiography – narrative of a person's life; a true story about a real person

Essay – a short literary composition that reflects the author's outlook or point

Owner's manual (also Instruction manual, User's guide) – an instructional book or booklet that is supplied with consumer products such as vehicles, home appliances, firearms, toys and computer peripherals

Journalism – reporting on news and current events

Memoir – factual story that focuses on a significant relationship between the writer and a person, place, or object; reads like a short novel

Narrative nonfiction/personal narrative – factual information about a significant event presented in a format which tells a story

Reference book

Self-help book

Textbook – authoritative and detailed factual description of a topic.

Subjects

There are also many subjects covered by nonfiction books. Which subject(s) does YOUR book deal with?

Architecture

Art

Biography

Body, Mind & Spirit

Business & Economics

Computers

Cooking

Crafts & Hobbies

Education

Family & Relationships

Games

Gardening

Health

History

House

Humor

Languages

Law

Literary

Math

Medical

Music

Nature

Performing Arts

Pets

Philosophy

Photography

Poetry

Political Science

Psychology

Reference

Religion

Science

Self-help

Social Science

Sports

Study Aids

Technology

Fiction vs Nonfiction

Transportation

Travel

True Crime

How Long Is A Book?

How many pages should your nonfiction book be? We don't know. It depends on what you have to say in writing and how you want to say it in writing. Some books are short, some books are hundreds of pages, some may even be longer. My books tend to be short, and to the point. Why? Because most people have a short attention span and, today, they may not want to wade through a 600-page book of nonfiction. That's why I write books that are often around 100 pages, are easy to read and easy to understand. Because MY audience likes it that way. YOUR audience may be different. Who's YOUR audience? Who are YOU writing for? Would they prefer a shorter book or a longer book?

What's the answer to the question of how many pages should your book be? That's like asking, "How long is a string?" It's as long as it needs to be. It's the same with a book. Your book will be as long as it will be.

And if you have like 1,000 pages, you might want to turn it into several books; a series, or volume 1, volume 2, volume 3 etc. I've done that too.

Let's Get Started

Assuming you have committed to writing (and finishing) your book, you're ready to get started

Under Pressure

Newbie authors put themselves under a lot of pressure. As a beginner author you are inexperienced, insecure, and in over your head. And you'll be that way until you write, and finish, your manuscript. This is normal. This is OK. Here's a little insight which can help you overcome or set aside those feelings of fear and thoughts of being unworthy and/or not up to the task.

It's not about you, it's about the story. You are just the messenger, bringing the story and/or facts and figures and details to the reader. You are the messenger. The delivery person.

It's not about you, it's about the book.

You do NOT have to be the best writer the world has ever seen. Yes, you can (and will) be less than perfect. It's your first draft and it doesn't have to be perfect. And it won't be. Neither are you. Neither am I. Nobody is.

Your book only needs to be interesting and reasonably readable. Let that be your standard.

Just do it. Make the commitment to do your book. Stop worrying about doing it and do it. It's the doing of it that's important, not the expertise and experience of you the messenger. Relax. Take a deep breath. You can do this. Become the messenger. Get started.

Title

What's the first thing to do? Figure out a good title. What's the main point of your book? That depends on what you are writing about, and why. For instance, a neighbor of mine wants to write a book about his life. And his life is REMARKABLE. He is half black/half white. And, as soon as he was born, his father wanted to kill him. He had a very difficult life and grew up in a bad neighborhood and escaped death (and jail) numerous times. In his 20's he miraculously turned his life around and became a successful gospel rapper (yes, really). He now spends his life being good to others and inspiring them with his music and deeds. The working title for his book is: ½ Breed (or as I suggested: Half-Breed). Along with my female Jewish Eskimo friend's book, his nonfiction book is worthy of being written. They are both unique books, inspirational in the extreme, and will be incredibly interesting to read. These 2 books MUST be written! And published. And they deserve to have great titles.

Sometimes you just can't come up with a good title in the beginning. Sometimes it's a huge headache. Sometimes it takes days or weeks to come up with a title. It's frustrating. Sometimes you easily come up with the perfect title. If you can't come up with the "perfect" title right now that's OK; just call it *something* so you can organize everything. It's called a working title. You can always change the title before publication.

And, as soon as you give your book a working title, make sure you immediately look up that title on the internet. How? I enter the exact title in quotes into the search engine and add the word "book". Why? To see if someone has written a book with that title and not just an article or a headline for a story. If a book comes up with your exact title, the title is already taken and you will have to change yours. Yes, it's always disappointing to discover that your brilliant "perfect" title is already taken. My original title for THIS book was already taken – so I had to change it around a little. Welcome to being an author.

The perfect title is not easy to come up with. It's the author's first obstacle or as I look at it, the author's first opportunity.

Covers

Yes, your book cover is important. Especially the front cover. It should portray the subject in a way that's attention-getting and, hopefully, pleasing. Your cover should make people want to buy – and read – your book.

Regarding the front and back covers you can do them now, do them later, let your publisher do them, or pay someone to design them. When I do my title I usually do a simple quick "working cover". The front cover. It takes me a few hours. And then I print it out so I can look at it and have it motivate me. My printed simple working front cover makes my book "real", at least to me. I look at the cover often and it motivates me to write - and finish - the book.

However, do not let the cover(s) delay the writing of the book! Start writing. Start writing now.

The Outline

Now that you have a working title, next, go get a legal pad. Or a blank page of typewriter paper. Or three. And a pen. Why? Because you need to outline your book - BEFORE you write it. Why? You do an outline so you know where you're going, where you've been, and where you are when you are writing your book.

On the legal pad, I first enter the main ideas for the book; which will later become the Chapters of the book. On the legal pad, I enter the ideas as they occur to me - I will reorganize and put the items in order later. The objective of the outline is to list ALL the things in the book that you want to have, or ought to have, in your book, all the things that you want your readers to read. This outline will become the basis, the plan, the blueprint, for what's in your book.

I spend time doing the outline. Hours. Days. Weeks. In the beginning the outline is always a mess. Things in the outline list are out of order, things are missing, things have to be taken out, or added. Take your time doing your outline, it will make your book easier to write and easier to finish. The more complete you make your outline, the easier it will be to write the book.

When you write a nonfiction book (or a fiction book)

you don't just sit down and write it. Why not? Because you will likely get stuck – often – and this may cause you to give up writing the book entirely. You need to do an outline because it's better to know what major points you want to make, and the order in which you write them; i.e. where you're going, where you've been, and where you are. The outline is a necessary guide. A necessary blueprint. A necessary plan. A good outline avoids many of the disasters of trying to write a book.

Author A.J Jacobs states: "I am a big fan of outlining. I write an outline. Then a slightly more detailed outline. Then another with even more detail. Sentences form, punctuation is added, and eventually it all turns into a book."

And, if you don't want to use a pen and legal pad yes you can use your electronic device to do the outline ... and to write your book. Yes, I write my books on my computer. But I personally prefer to do the outline on a legal pad. With a pen. Old school.

Research

Some books may require a lot of research. Some may not.

How much research you need to do depends on your topic and subject matter. If it's a history you may need to do a lot of research. If it's a biography, or a self-help book, research may or may not be needed. Most of my books do not require a lot of research as they are mostly opinion, based on my vast life experience and keen always correct observation. (yes, that's humor!)

If you do need to do research, the internet is an excellent source – just be careful – make sure the source is a legitimate source. You might also use your local library for research on your topic.

And, if you do use someone's published original research, the information is copyrighted – ask for permission to use it and/or give full credit to the source, either in the body of the book or in footnotes.

The 3 Stages Of Writing A Book

The 3 basic stages of writing a book are:

1. the First Draft

2. the final manuscript

3. publishing

The First Draft is the actual writing of your manuscript - for the first time. The First Draft is the main focus of THIS book: "How To Write Your Nonfiction Book". Without doing a First Draft you cannot get to the second and third stages ... and cannot complete your book.

The second stage (the final manuscript) entails rewriting and editing and proofreading the First Draft. You are redoing, rewriting, editing, proofreading and/or "polishing" the First Draft. Why? Because the First Draft is always not "all that it could be" or all you want it to be; and needs work re grammar, chapter order, structure and several other things – in order to make it more readable and more comprehensible to your readers.

The last phase of the final manuscript stage is

proofreading, i.e. fixing spelling errors, grammar errors etc.

The third stage is publishing. This involves choosing book size, formatting, final covers, book design, printing, marketing, promotion and lots of other complicated things. For right now **ignore this stage!** If you don't you will likely be overwhelmed and never start or finish your book! Once you finish your First Draft, and the final manuscript, you will then deal with the third stage.

As a beginning author, it is very helpful not to look at your book as an entire project, from the writing to the publishing. It is too daunting to look at the whole project. By daunting I mean "seeming difficult to deal with in anticipation; intimidating". Instead, look at your book project as "parts", not as a whole.

Concentrate on starting the book, writing the book, getting the First Draft done and finished. That is your first goal, your ONLY goal.

Writing The Book – First Draft

Do your outline. Once you have finished your outline you are ready to start writing the First Draft of your book.

When you are writing do not worry about style, spelling, punctuation, margins et al. Just write down everything you want to say. Use complete sentences if appropriate. The objective right now is to write the book – the first draft of the book. The First Draft is often lousy. Bad spelling mistakes, bad/no/incorrect punctuation, disorganized. Ugh, a mess. Not to worry, that's normal, and that's what rewriting is for. I often have to do 3-4 drafts (rewrites) and get someone to proofread it until I get a "final draft", a final manuscript.

The objective now is to get everything down on paper (or on your computer). Or, as some authors prefer, dictate it. Do your book. All of it. In your own style. Later you will fix what needs to be fixed. Right now, and for the next few weeks/months, just write. Make a mess. I make a mess using Microsoft Word, on my computer.

Write everything you can on your subject, no matter what it is, following and expanding on your outline as you go. You will add stuff and remove stuff later, when you rewrite and edit your manuscript.

This will be your first draft. Your initial manuscript. This is the most creative, fulfilling and fun part of writing a book!

The Objective

The objective of writing a book is to write the book. Yes, it sounds redundant but it's not. The ONLY focus at this stage is to write the book. Not to get it published. Not the cover art. Not what your friends and family think of it. Not how to market it, or publicize it. First, write the book! All your concentration should be on writing the book, nothing else. Your first objective is to write your book - and finish your book. Your main objective is to produce a **First Draft**. Nothing else. Everything else is a distraction, a potentially deadly distraction. Beware!

At this stage do not worry about editing or proofreading your book. The first objective is to get everything down on paper (or your computer) or tape recording. The rest comes later. And, in case you were wondering, it usually takes me about a month or so to write (and rewrite a book). And my books are short. I usually spend about 4 hours a day at it (everybody's schedule is different). The first draft of this book took me 10 days. Yes, I wrote the first draft quickly. I was able to do that because this book is based on experience – mine – and I was able to write most of it from memory. Getting all this stuff out of my head and onto paper was not easy but it was a worthy challenge and worth doing.

Regarding doing a book, the easiest and most fun and most rewarding part is the writing of it, so enjoy it.

The first draft is the "manuscript". After the rewriting and editing and proofreading stages and you are satisfied with all that you have a "final manuscript". As for the rewriting, editing, proofreading, formatting, publishing, marketing, etc don't worry about it, all that comes later, AFTER your First Draft.

Though this book does not deal in depth with things beyond the First Draft (if it did the book would be 1,000 pages) there are plenty of other good books you can read that deal with that – when you get to those stages.

First, do the First Draft!

Chapters

How do you write a book? You write a book one word at a time. Put several words together and you can make a sentence. Several sentences make a paragraph. Paragraphs make up a page. Pages make up a chapter. And chapters make up a book. It's a process. A manageable process, when you break it down into small, manageable steps.

Words. Words become sentences, become paragraphs, becomes chapters - becomes a book. Anyone can write (or say) one or more words at a time. Yes, even you!

Give Yourself A Break

It's hard enough to write a book. Writing is hard, writing for hours each day is hard. When doing a book I write (or sit there) for 4 hours a day. That's all I can do, attention and energy wise. You may be different. Maybe you will be able to write for 6 hours a day. Or 2 hours. Or 1 hour. It's OK, write until you have to stop.

When writing please plan to take a break. Several breaks if you need them. I normally take a break when the ideas stop coming, when I get stuck, or after I write something brilliant, or have to use the bathroom. Or eat. Or make a cup of coffee (which I am having right now!)

Taking a break(s) during your writing is like allowing yourself to digest a meal after eating. It's healthy! If you have to, set an alarm to go off every 2 hours, or 1 hour, if only to make you get up and walk around, and get the blood flowing.

A short break can stimulate your brain.

Schedule permitting, I usually sit down to write at about 7:30 AM and continue until 11:30 AM or so. Sometimes I go back to my computer after lunch for an hour or so. I do this every day. I get up from my chair every hour or so, sometimes every half-hour. Naps work great for me too. And sometimes I take a break for a whole day. Or a whole week. I may not be writing during a break but I'm still working - my book is percolating - in my brain and subconscious.

Regarding times to write, everyone is different, with different schedules, different sleep/wake cycles etc. You have to make your own schedule and adapt it to your life outside of writing. And you have to give yourself a break. Literally.

To me writing is like a job, a fantastic part-time fun satisfying job. For me, writing IS a break, a break from the realities, pressures and difficulties of daily living.

Editing Your Work

I don't edit much as I write. I don't stop to edit much except the spelling of a word (if I catch it).

When you write, finish the sentence. Finish the paragraph. Finish the page. Finish the chapter. You will edit later. Yes, I try to correct my spelling as I write (thank God for spellcheck!) but I do not heavily edit or rewrite when I am writing new stuff. That comes later.

The major editing and rewriting will come AFTER you finish writing your manuscript – after you have the First Draft. If you do heavy editing as you write you will soon realize that you are "too close" to the writing and will *make* mistakes, not correct them.

If you do want to edit your work as you are writing your book, I suggest you do what I call "light editing". This type of editing is basic, mainly reading over what you wrote before and correcting the simple stuff; misspellings, obvious grammar mistakes, etc. This type of editing is best done the next day. Wait a day. Or 3. Or a week. Then go back and edit – with a fresh eye. The real rewriting and editing is tackled after you have the First Draft.

Writing Tools

Today, many writers write their book on a computer. Some use a pen and paper. Some even use a typewriter. Some use a tape recorder. These are writing tools. Yes, it's more efficient to write a book on a computer; because it's easier to format, edit and send the manuscript.

Use whatever writing tool(s) work for you. Whatever non-electronic device you use you can always later transcribe the words and turn them into a manuscript, or have them transcribed, it just takes longer and may cost money.

The objective of writing a book is to write the book. Another major objective is to finish the book. H-o-w you do those things is not critical, DOING them is critical! In the end, as an art form, it doesn't matter how you write, only that you write. I don't care if you use chalk on a blackboard, just be careful nobody erases your work.

You can write standing up, sitting down, lying down or standing on your head. And use whatever writing tools you want/have to use.

Write the book. Finish the book.

Work Habits

You may not have developed your book writing habits yet. That's OK. Writing habits vary from author to author and are very personalized. Some writers write in the early morning, some late at night. Some sit at the computer all day, some only an hour or two. Some writers try to write every day, some are not as consistent. Some authors write in their underwear, some may even write naked! Victor Hugo, when he was facing a tight schedule for his famed novel The Hunchback of Notre Dame, instructed his valet to confiscate all his clothes so he wouldn't be able to leave the house.

Not to worry, you will find out what habits work for y-o-u. But until you do, your writing habits may frustrate you, make you laugh or make you cry or want to give up but writing habits are a matter of creativity and what works for YOU. You will find out the habits that work for you. These habits may be a bit strange, like looking out the window for a half-hour. Or laying on the couch. It looks like goofing off but you may be thinking great thoughts, not goofing off.

I usually start the day's writing session by looking over what I wrote the day before. That puts me in a writing mode and I am then able to just pick up where I left off and continue writing fresh stuff, based on my outline. Then, every few days I go back over everything, reading what I wrote and do some simple fixes where needed, i.e. where it's obvious that I left out a word etc. That works for me, it may not be good for YOUR writing methods.

You will develop your own methods and habits. As long as they are not harmful (or illegal) make your writing habits work for you, and help you write your book(s).

Writing habits are personal. Very personal. And some people in your life may not accept or understand your writing habits. These people may include your spouse or your kids or anyone who interrupts your work. As a writer you do not want to be disturbed unless it's an emergency. "The house is on fire! Get out!" "OK, I'll leave as soon as I finish this paragraph."

When you are writing you are CREATING. Yes, when you are writing your book you are a creative artist. Like a painter, only with words.

I realize that many authors also have a job or family members to take care of and they don't have the luxury of writing whenever or wherever they get the urge. Nobody said it was easy to be a writer. I read that the famous American author, Mario Puzo (The Godfather) worked full time - at the Post Office. He would get up extra early and write before he went to work. I guess that habit worked OK for him, wouldn't you say?

Toni Morrison is also known to take a nap after lunch. Me too!

George Orwell often wrote at night, but he wrote at all other times of day, as well.

It is said that some writers, like Hemingway, Charles

Dickens, Virginia Woolf, Lewis Carroll, and Philip Roth wrote standing up! Others wrote lying down.

And, when you are writing, if you are not writing your book on your cellphone, turn it off! Writing a book is distracting enough, no added distractions are necessary.

How do I work? What are MY writing habits? OK, I'll tell you. Yes, you can skip this section if you want to.

I write in the morning. Because I am an early morning person. I get up early and am most "awake" in the first few hours of the day. I eat breakfast and go to my desk at home by 8 AM. I try to sit there for at least 3 hours (including breaks), whether I write anything or not. Usually I am able to write something (hopefully it's not too horrible) because I have something to say. Something important. Something worth saying. That's why I am writing the book. When I write I do not need to write "perfectly" – I will fix everything when I rewrite, edit and proofread it. I found that I am not good at writing at night. So I avoid it. I tried it several times and found that my writing was so lousy it was worthless so I stopped writing at night. I am a day writer. An early morning writer. And, partly as a result of paying attention to WHEN I write well, I am a GOOD writer!

While I am working I am not overly distracted by my surroundings. The TV is usually on, the phone may ring, somebody may be talking to me – I hear NOTHING. When I am writing I am in the zone, the writing zone. At that moment nothing is more important than writing. Self-centered? Egotistical? Selfish? Yes. Writers are artists and all artists are self-indulgent when they are creating. Watch out for addictions. Addictions include alcohol, drugs, food, sex and other things creative people tend to get drawn to.

Don't add any new ones.

When I am doing a book I try to write for about 4 hours every day. I look forward to it. I am drawn to it, like a moth to a flame. It's a part of me, a creative outlet, a reason to get out of bed in the morning, a reason to live.

How do I start my writing day? I wake up, eat a little breakfast, make some coffee, put on some clothes and go to my computer. I look at my outline, boot up my laptop and continue writing based on my outline. Or, when my outline is complete and already written into my First Draft, I read what I wrote the day before. It's now a day later and reading what I previously wrote gives me a fresh look at it. I do a little simple quick proofreading and editing on that section (not heavy rewriting or editing). This puts me in "the writing zone".

Note: at this point, right here in this book, after a week or so I ran out of outline stuff. So I stopped writing for the moment and couldn't think of something new to write. Am I stumped? Is this writer's block? Yes. And no. I have faith that I will soon be able to continue, as soon as I add more stuff to my outline or can think of something else to add to the book. I am also prepared to sit and look at my screen, at a blank page, for 2 or 3 hours that day and write little or nothing. Or take a walk. You get stuck. It happens. And sometimes I leave off writing my book for several days before continuing. This allows the book – and me – to percolate. To renew. To become fresh.

Yes, to be an author you need patience. And faith. Lots of it. The sincere and strong desire to write your book will help drive you to write it, and finish it, and help you overcome any and all obstacles.

The point of this chapter on writing habits is to make you more comfortable having writing habits. Your own writing habits. It's a question of whatever works. For y-o-u. No matter how weird a writer's habits may be, they are part of our weirdness, and are supposed to help get the crazy creative job done.

Sharing

What about telling people that you are writing a book? What about sharing your book or book idea with friends and family? Or co-workers? You are excited about your book and it's a natural and normal thing to want to do. It can also be disappointing.

I once wrote a screenplay. I thought it was a wonderful screenplay. I was very excited and very pleased with my accomplishment. When I finished writing it I showed it to some of my family members. Their response? They didn't know what a screenplay was, had no interest in reading it, and simply said nice polite things about me writing a screenplay. Basically, I got a blank look from them. My friends had the same response. My family and friends responded as if I had a hobby that they didn't understand, or were not interested in. I also had another friend, a neighbor, who was very supportive. This friend loved my work, read every book manuscript I wrote and even helped me proofread them. I greatly appreciated that.

In general, do not expect other people in your life to automatically be excited about your book. They might be. And that's a wonderful thing. And they might not be. Some may even be mean. Or jealous. Or uncaring.

Most of my friends and family could care less about my books and do not want to read them or hear about them. That's often/sometimes the way it is. Writing is a lonely business. I got used to it. So will you. I learned who to share my writing with and who not to share my writing with. You will too. Make that OK.

Yes, you can share becoming an author with others, just do not expect them to be automatically excited and supportive. Like I said, they might be or they might not be. I'm just telling you in advance. No, I am not saying you should keep your writing and authordom a secret. Try sharing it. You will quickly find out who is truly interested and supportive and who is not. Do not hold it against those who seemingly don't care about your book. Don't take it personally. Maybe they were having a bad day. Or hate books.

As a writer, an author, you are writing for an audience, not your friends and family. If you have family and friends that support you you are lucky. Otherwise, if you want support or to share being an author and do not find it among your family and friends, join a local writer's group.

Getting Your Book Published

Books are normally published by publishing houses or by the author themselves (self-publishing). It is very difficult for an unknown author to get an established publishing house to publish their book. Unless you are already famous the probability of getting published by a major legitimate publishing house is near zero. So is getting a powerful high-level literary agent to negotiate your deal. Why? Because publishing is a business and a publishing house wants to make money, by selling books. Lots of books. And the easiest way to sell a lot of books is to publish and sell a book written by someone who is already well known, who already has a big following. It gives the publisher a built-in already existing potentially huge audience and customer base.

There are also subsidy publishing houses. You pay them to publish your book. They offer many needed services but it will cost you. Expect to pay up to several thousand dollars or more to have your book published by a subsidy press.

Otherwise you probably will have to self-publish your book. Not to worry, there are several good inexpensive self-publishing companies to help you through the process.

Don't worry about the publishing stuff now. Forget it even exists. Why? Because if you don't write, and finish, your book manuscript, getting published will not be an issue, because it will not happen. Write your book!

Proofreading

Yes, proofreading is a must. Your book must contain correct spelling and correct punctuation and flow properly. It's a reflection of you.

Yes, while/after editing you can do proofreading. I often do 2-3 proofreadings after the first draft.

The writing order of a book:

Write

Rewrite

Edit

Proofread

I happen to be a good speller. As good a speller as I am, when proofreading I ALWAYS find errors, in spelling, in punctuation, in clarity of thought. Always.

When proofreading, I wait a few days between proofreadings. Though I proofread my manuscript several times over a few days or weeks it's not enough. Why? Because I wrote the stuff; I'm too close to it and I don't catch ALL the errors.

After I have finished the manuscript, and proofread it several times, I let it sit. I don't touch it. For how long?

Usually for a few days, or a week or so. Why? So I can look at it again, with a fresh eye. Then, after I re-read the whole thing, and fix the errors I find, I get someone to proofread it. Why? Because they will find errors I missed. Because a good outside proofreader will make my book BETTER! And save me from embarrassment when the reader sees a glaring mistake I missed and didn't fix. Use a final outside person to proofread your final manuscript! It does not have to be a professional but it does have to be someone proficient in reading and fixing English (assuming your book is in English). I learned this the hard way. For one of my early book manuscripts, after proofreading it 3-4 times, I did not use a final outside proofreader. After the book was published I found NUMEROUS errors in sentence structure and punctuation. I was very upset. My writing is also a reflection of me, and these errors did not give the reader (or me) a good impression. The mistakes were now in the book – forever! I was horrified. And embarrassed. I learned my lesson.

A final proofreading, by someone other than yourself, is a must.

Copyright

Once you have totally finished writing your book and have a final manuscript, you'll want to get it copyrighted, at the Library of Congress in Washington, D.C. If your publisher doesn't offer to do this, you can do it all online yourself. The official U.S. copyright website walks you through doing it and it's not overly complicated. And it's not expensive either. Do it. And, no, you don't have to take a trip to Washington, D.C., you can do it online or by mail.

I am not a Copyright Attorney (or any other kind of attorney) but, according to Authorhouse.com, under U.S. copyright law, your work is protected as soon as you put the pen to paper. Copyright is based on your creative authorship and is not dependent on any formal agreement with a book publisher or self publishing company, although registration with the U.S. Copyright Office is beneficial.

Copyright Registration allows you, as an author, a higher level of security and confidence when it comes to protecting your work. When you register your work with the U.S. Copyright office, you create a public record of your authorship. Even though you are protected from the moment you start writing, you'll have to register your work with the Copyright Office to be officially recognized as the copyright holder in a court of law."

Again, I am not a lawyer but I believe if you ever want/need to sue in court for copyright infringement, or stop someone from using your copyrighted information (injunction), you need to have officially registered your work and have an existing official copyright, issued by the Copyright Office of the Library of Congress. This is the best legal protection for your book, your "baby".

How do you copyright your work? From LegalZoom.com: "To register a book or other creative work, simply go to copyright.gov, the website set up by the Library of Congress. There is an online portal to register copyrights for photographs, sculptures and written works. Fill out the form, pay the fee and you are registered."

Congratulations!

When you finish writing the first draft of your book and write "The End" you will feel a huge sense of accomplishment. Your book is finished! At least for the moment. After you do all the rewrites and editing and proofreading and are finally satisfied enough with your final draft you'll have a Final Manuscript – and you will have truly finished your book! Great! You will feel another huge sense of accomplishment. And possibly a huge letdown. Your book is done. Finished. Your "baby" has been born. Be prepared to suffer a brief postpartum depression, whether you are male or female or whatever your sexual identity is. Give it a week if necessary to get over the powerful feelings of finishing your book.

What's the best way to overcome the postpartum depression caused by finishing your book? Write another one!

Your First Draft is done! Your basic book is done! Whew, it was a lot of work and a lot of frustration, but it is a fantastic accomplishment. Congratulations, you are now an author!!!

Recap

Here's the steps to get organized, stay organized ... and write your book.

• Have something worth writing about

• Find your motivation. Why are you writing the book?

• What's your idea?

• Hurry up and wait

• How will you write your book? By hand, computer, dictation?

• Working title

• Front cover (optional)

• Do an outline

• Do the research (if necessary)

• Write the book – First Draft

Then comes

• Rewriting

• Editing

- Proofreading
- Final Draft
- Copyright
- Publication

Yes, now that you finished reading this book you're ready to start writing your own book. Yes, it's going to be unique, exciting and special. And you get to shape it, mold it, own it! You are going to write a book. YOUR book. You are going to be an author. Yes, you CAN do it.

Famous Quotes

"Writing, to me, is simply thinking through my fingers" - Isaac Asimov

"It took me fifteen years to discover I had no talent for writing, but I couldn't give it up because by that time I was too famous." – Robert Benchley

"Writing is its own reward." – Henry Miller

"Everybody walks past a thousand story ideas every day. The good writers are the ones who see five or six of them. Most people don't see any." – Orson Scott Card

"I don't need an alarm clock. My ideas wake me." —Ray Bradbury

"It's none of their business that you have to learn to write. Let them think you were born that way." — Ernest Hemingway

"A professional writer is an amateur who didn't quit." —Richard Bach

"Good writing is rewriting." —Truman Capote

"Writing is easy. All you have to do is cross out the wrong words." - Mark Twain

"The first draft of anything is shit." - Ernest

Hemingway

"Writing became such a process of discovery that I couldn't wait to get to work in the morning: I wanted to know what I was going to say." - Sharon O'Brien

"I'm not a very good writer, but I'm an excellent rewriter." - James Michener

"Every writer I know has trouble writing." - Joseph Heller

"What no spouse of a writer can ever understand is that a writer is working when he's staring out of the window." – unknown

"It is impossible to discourage the real writers — they don't give a damn what you say, they're going to write." - Sinclair Lewis

"The book's idea or theme or meaning has been stirring about in your consciousness for months and probably years. When the idea first hits you you feel enormously stimulated and heightened. Then you wish you could get away from it, but now nothing but death can separate you from it. It's no use. Now everything else in your life takes second place or fades out of your consciousness altogether. Clothes are unimportant, letters go unanswered for days or even weeks, parties you regard with a lackluster eye, travel is a lure to be avoided like death, for it is ruin to the sustained rhythm of your work day." – Edna Ferber

"Writing did not save my life... but it has continued to do what it always has done: it makes my life a brighter and more pleasant place. Writing isn't about making money, getting famous, getting dates, getting laid, or making friends. In the end, it's about enriching the lives of those who will read your work, and enriching your own life, as well." - Stephen King

THE END

Free excerpts from some of my books ...

"Step It Up: The Quest For Success"

This book is dedicated to everyone who is "stuck" in their quest for success

Introduction

So, you have a dream. You want to achieve something. You want to achieve something that means a great deal to you. But you can't. It just isn't happening. So you get frustrated or upset. Or depressed. Because you can't achieve your goal. It's too hard, or too costly, or it's taking too long, or it looks like it's impossible. It just isn't happening.

You are thwarted, stuck, unable to proceed, unable to succeed.

Welcome to life. Real life. Welcome to trying to achieve something, something you really want in your life, and not achieving your goal. Whether it's a career or a relationship or a personal goal ... you are struggling ... and not achieving your goal. And it sucks.

So do you give up? Quit? You could. You could give up, you could quit. It's certainly easier than continuing to struggle. Do you give up your heart's desire and settle for whatever (or whomever) you can get? You could. Giving up is easier. Quitting is easier. But if you give up now you will be a quitter. A loser. And you don't want to be a loser. NOBODY wants to be a loser!

So, what do you do? What do you do now?

You don't give up, you try again. One more time. Why will this time be any different? Because this time you are going to increase your odds of winning. This time you are going to Step It Up! Step it up? How do you step it up? You start by reading this book. This book can make you stronger, can help you remove or overcome the obstacles in your way, and can help you get what you really want.

This book is going to motivate you, inspire you, and show you how to Step It Up--and move closer to your goal. Read it. Do it. Live it.

Chapter 2
Failure

OK, first let's talk about failure. Failure, what is it? Failure is where and when you are failing to achieve your chosen goal. Failure, believe it or not, is normal. Sometimes it takes several tries to accomplish something. Ask any scientist or inventor or business owner or actor ("Yes, such and such became a star overnight--after 10 years in the business.")

Failure does not have to be PERMANENT. Unless you make it permanent. Failure is temporary. It's the place you get stuck in ... until you get unstuck, until you succeed.

How do you get "unstuck"? Sometimes it just happens. Sometimes it doesn't. Sometimes you get stuck in "stuck". That's when you Step It Up. That's when you put forth MORE effort. 100%. 110%. Or you do something different to move forward. It's when you try another avenue to get to your goal. Try something different. The something different to try is Stepping It Up.

Chapter 3
Successful Failures

Don't ever think that YOU are the only failure. Or that you will never succeed. Here are some good examples of successful failures.

Richard Branson

net worth: $4.6 billion

If you were to meet him in his teens, you would have bet that Richard Branson would be a failure. Branson had poor reading and math skills, dropped out of high-school and is proud to admit he's dyslexic all his life. In spite of all this he became a billionaire, a knight, a philanthropist and a media and transportation mogul.

Branson has a long history of failures. Virgin Cola, Virgin Vodka, Virgin Vie, Virgin Brides, Virgin Clothing, Virgin Cars, Virgin Digital all failed. Branson's response? *"Learn from failure. If you are an entrepreneur and your first venture wasn't a success, welcome to the club!"*

J.K. Rowling
Net worth: $1 billion

Before she published the Harry Potter novel she was penniless, divorced, depressed, raising a child on her own and going to school. The first Harry Potter book was rejected 9 times. Overcoming enormous personal obstacles, Rowling went from being on welfare to being a billionaire. In five years. How did she do it? By investing a lot of hard work and a lot of determination.

Albert Einstein

Einstein did not speak until he was four and did not read until he was seven, causing his teachers and parents to think he was mentally handicapped and slow to learn.

Abraham Lincoln

He started numerous failed businesses, went bankrupt twice, and was defeated in 26 campaigns he made for public office. Yet he ended up the President of the United States.

Walt Disney

Walt Disney had many personal failures. He was fired by a newspaper editor because, "he lacked imagination and had no good ideas." Really? After that, Disney started a number of businesses that didn't last too long and ended with bankruptcy and failure.

Colonel Sanders

Kentucky Fried Chicken. Sanders had a hard time selling his chicken at first. In fact, his famous secret chicken recipe was rejected 1,009 times before a restaurant accepted it. Over 1,000 failures!

Thomas Edison

In his early years, teachers told Edison he was "too stupid to learn anything." Work was no better, as he was fired from his first two jobs ... for not being productive enough. He persevered and became America's most famous inventor.

Michael Jordan

Perhaps the best professional basketball player of all time. He was cut from his high school basketball team.

The Beatles

When they were first starting out, a record company rejected them saying "We don't like their sound, and guitar music is on the way out". The Beatles went on to become the most popular band in history.

Stephen King

His first book, the iconic thriller Carrie, received 30 rejections, finally causing King to give up and throw it in the trash. His wife fished it out and encouraged him to resubmit it, and the rest is history, making King one of the best-selling authors of all time. 30 rejections?

Henry Ford

Henry Ford went broke five times before he became the founder of the Ford Motor Company and the "Father of the Automobile".

Vincent Van Gogh

Van Gogh sold only one painting in his life, to a friend, for a very small amount of money. Van Gogh was never an artistic success during his life, and sometimes went starving. The very definition of the starving artist. Van Gogh created over 800 works. Today, some of his paintings sell for hundreds of millions of dollars. Each.

Marilyn Monroe

Told by modeling agents that she should instead consider being a secretary. Marilyn Monroe became a superstar pin-up model and actress who, today, still invokes the sensuality and glamour of Hollywood.

Dr. Seuss

The best-selling author of children's books had his first book rejected. 27 times.

Elvis Presley

As one of the best-selling recording artists of all time, Elvis Presley is a household name in music even many years after his death. In 1954, when Elvis was still an unknown, the manager of the Grand Ole Opry fired Elvis Presley after his first performance, telling him, "You ain't goin' nowhere, son. You ought to go back to drivin' a truck." Needless to say, Elvis persevered in his music career, becoming "The King of Rock and Roll".

Let these people be a lesson to you! Even the BEST failed -- before they succeeded!

Like all the people above, you just need to step it up!

"Step It Up – The quest for success". For more guidance on how to Step It Up, and succeed, read the book.

"Stories of A Lifetime"
(extraordinary events in
an extraordinary life)

A Real Case Of ESP

It was a very hot summer the year I turned 17. Broiling hot. Roasting hot. There were no beaches within hundreds of miles of my hometown. However, my friend Bill's aunt lived in Asbury Park, NJ. Right near the beach. She invited Bill to visit her for a few days. Bill invited me. I had never been to Asbury Park, NJ before. The three of us went; Bill, me, and the Greyhound bus.

We were welcomed at the aunt's house; we had a place to stay and the Atlantic Ocean nearby. It was cooler already. To get to the beach and back we could simply catch a shuttle bus that regularly made the thirty-forty minute trip. The next morning Bill and I packed up our suntan lotion and caught the shuttle to the beach. In the late afternoon we returned to the aunt's house for dinner. The third day, we met a beautiful blonde on the shuttle bus and talked to her all the way out to the beach. The next morning she was once again on the same bus that we rode. She was exceptionally pretty, very nice and about the same age as Bill and I. She told us her first and last name, a little about herself and the name (but not the number) of the street she lived on. It was a main street which ran for maybe ten miles through Asbury Park.

Later that evening, after dinner, Bill and I took a walk. We found ourselves on the same street where our new blonde friend lived. We laughed. Bill said we should go and visit her, except we didn't have the address only the street and the street was ten miles long. And there weren't any phonebooks anywhere around to look up her address, assuming she was even listed.

We kept walking. Block after block. Houses and apartment buildings lined both sides of the wide and long avenue. After about twenty minutes we came abreast of a nondescript medium sized apartment building. Suddenly, I stopped. I pointed my finger at the building and said, "She lives there."

Bill laughed. "Yeah, right" he said.

"No," I said emphatically, "she really does live right there."

Bill looked at the building. Then he looked me. Then he looked back at the building. "There's thousands of buildings on this street and she could be living in any one of them and you're telling me she lives in this building right here?"

"She lives here," I restated.

"Yeah, right. Let's just see", he said and walked up to the entrance of the building. I followed as he opened the door, stepped inside and went over to the tenant directory on the wall. He looked for her last name on the roster... and found it!

He turned to me with a strange look on his face. "This is her last name alright," he said. "But it's a common last name and the first name is different anyhow and maybe it ain't her."

"She lives here," I said.

Bill picked up the house phone, buzzed the apartment

and, when someone answered, asked for the girl by name.

The girl came to the phone.

It turned out that she lived with her mother. Right there in that building on that wide, long street in Asbury Park, New Jersey.

She was totally amazed that we found her.

So was I.

The Night We Saw A Real UFO

When I was 18 years old I saw a real UFO.

I wasn't the only one who saw it.

It was a typical, incredibly clear summer night in Binghamton, NY. There were a billion shining and twinkling stars overhead. Six or seven of us were over at my girlfriend's house, at the top of one of the big hills/little mountains that ringed the town. We were outside. Just fooling around. I don't know who first noticed something up in the sky but quickly we were all looking up to see. At first glance all there was to see was an airplane, not unusual due to the proximity of Broome County Airport. It had blinking lights like an airplane, flew like an airplane and was just an airplane. Flying southeast at maybe five thousand to ten thousand feet maximum. But then something weird happened. In a moment, as we continued to watch the airplane, something else started flying around it; circling it, darting back and forth.

Something very weird. A smaller object than the airliner. This smaller flying object didn't have normal airplane lights, it's lights didn't blink and it looked like the whole thing was lit from the inside. Like a bright little shooting star. But it wasn't a shooting star. And it wasn't making any of the normal aeronautical movements airplanes make. This thing darted, in a strange jerky motion. This flying object was awesome! It accelerated faster than anything I have ever seen on land, sea or sky. It turned at impossible angles. It stopped dead in the sky! It darted around the airplane. From one side to the other. From front to back. Like it was taking a really close-up look. We all watched, dumbfounded, our mouths gaping. "What the hell is that???", we astonishingly asked. "It sure ain't no airplane", someone stated. Maybe it's one of those weather balloons, another ventured. No way a balloon could fly like that, someone answered. A comet? A shooting star? Some kind of top secret new Air Force plane?

We continued to watch the object buzz the commercial airliner. After about three or four minutes of darting around the airplane the object just stopped, and hung there in the sky for a moment. Like it was gathering strength. Then, faster than any comet or shooting star, it sped from one end of the vast sky to the other... as fast as the eye could follow ... and disappeared.

undreds of people who had witnessed the event called the airport and the police for an explanation. It was reported on the local news and in the local newspaper.

No satisfactory explanation was ever given.

Man Kills Building

In L.A., at one time, being bored, I took a job with a company in a large three story cement building which housed approximately one hundred people. The company trained people how to trade commodities. I was one of the supervisors for the staff of sales people. Some of our sales staff were rather difficult and rough characters. Including Nick. Nick H. was the current Ultimate Fighting Champion of the World. In case you do not know what that is, it's organized two-man no-holds-barred brawling involving boxing, kickboxing and other martial arts. The two combatants keep fighting until one of them gives up. Or dies. As a person, Nick was a terrific guy ... who happened to have a very short fuse ... attached to an explosive and lethal arsenal of fighting skills. Besides being a great guy Nick was dangerous. Deadly. Scary.

Luckily, he liked me.

One day I was taking a break in the parking lot next to our building when suddenly the door burst open (actually the door burst right off its hinges) and Nick came storming out. He was very upset. One of the other supervisors followed him out through the door-less doorway. The young supervisor and Nick apparently had had a verbal confrontation that now threatened to possibly erupt into murder. Nick being the potential murderer. With tremendous restraint Nick walked away from the kid and ranted and raved around the parking lot, getting more and more angry by the second.

By now, there were a half-dozen people who had come out to see what was going on. Adrenaline pumping, I decided to cautiously approach him to find out what was wrong.

Before I could get any nearer Nick walked up close to the building.

And started to punch the cement building with all his considerable might and skill.

He was trying to kill the building! He hit the building so hard I saw it actually shudder! It moved! He kept on hitting the building. Harder and harder. He hit it so hard that one of the women from administration came out onto the third floor outer stairs; she said she had been inside, felt the building shudder, and thought it was an earthquake!

I stood there absolutely amazed. I had never seen anything like it. Neither had anyone else. I gently walked up to Nick and started gently talking to him. He told me he was upset because the 23-year-old supervisor was telling him how to sell, something Nick had been doing successfully for many years. It's what Nick did, between fights.

Nick is telling me all this while he is still ranting and raving and still punching the building. I noticed his knuckles were all bloody (he didn't notice) and told him maybe he should leave the building alone, it was probably dead by now and he didn't need to break his hands as that would maybe hamper his fighting career.

Luckily, he liked me.

He stopped killing the building. I walked him around the parking lot to cool down and then took him back inside to wash the cuts on his hands. We both noticed the door, torn off its hinges, now propped up against the wall. "Did I do that?" Nick asked. I just looked at him.

Workmen arrived shortly and installed a new door.

Nick, legitimately the toughest man in the world, shortly calmed down and went back to work.

I, either the bravest or the stupidest supervisor in the world, shortly resumed breathing and went back to work.

The near-mortally injured building also recovered ... and is still standing today.

Incredible. And true. Want to read more incredible and true stories? Get the book.

Books by Andrew Lawrence

Step It Up: The Quest For Success

Life Changers: 10 true secrets that will change
your life

The Happiness Transformation

Discover Your Life Purpose in 30 Minutes

MONEY - The Basics

Stories Of A Lifetime

Rants In My Pants: outrage in the new America

Rants In My Pants Volume 2

Parties In My Pants

Parties In My Pants Volume 2

How To Get A Job

Soul Sex: The Ultimate Pleasure

Glimmers Of Hope

Break Into Showbiz

How To Solve Customer Service Problems
– Fast

Andrew Lawrence

Beat Your Fatigue
The 65-Year-Old Teenager
How To Thrive After 65
Wall Street - The Real Deal